CLEANING
HINTS & TIPS

CLEANING

HINTS & TIPS

CINDY HARRIS

RYLAND PETERS & SMALL

LONDON • NEW YORK

Senior Designer Barbara Zuñiga
Commissioning Editor Nathan Joyce
Production Controller Meskerem Berhane
Picture Manager Christina Borsi
Art Director Leslie Harrington
Editorial Director Julia Charles

First published in 2005
This edition published in 2014
by Ryland Peters & Small
20–21 Jockey's Fields
London WC1R 4BW
and
519 Broadway, 5th Floor
New York, NY 10012
www.rylandpeters.com

10 9 8 7 6 5 4 3 2

Text © Cindy Harris 2005, 2014
Design and photographs
© Ryland Peters & Small 2014

ISBN 978-1-84975-578-8

A CIP record for this book is
available from the British Library.

Library of Congress CIP data has been
applied for.

Printed and bound in China

CONTENTS

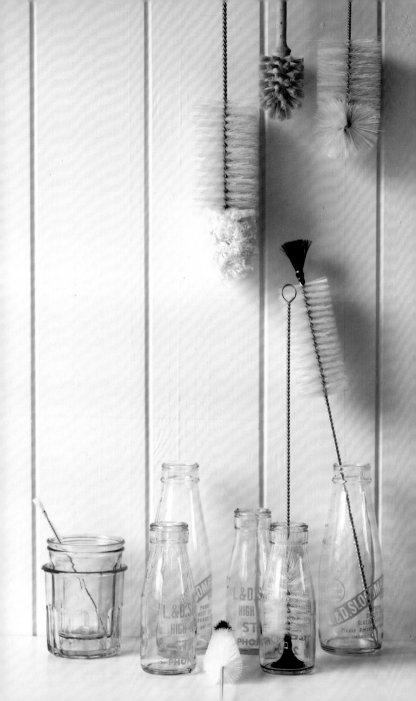

INTRODUCTION

Your home should be a place in which you can relax, feel comfortable and restore yourself from the stresses and strains of the day. Only by keeping your home in top condition can it become a refuge for you and your family. A neglected home becomes a chaotic and unhappy place, whereas a home that is well kept will not only be a pleasure to come back to, but it will improve your mental wellbeing – if your home is in order, the rest of your life will feel manageable.

Think of shiny baths and sinks, sparkling taps/faucets and a grime-free oven. Clean windows and scrubbed floors. All you need to get your home looking this good are the tools, the know-how and a routine that works for you and your family. This book will give you all these things, including a beautifully clean home that will sparkle.

GETTING YOUR
HOME IN ORDER

SIMPLE HOME MANAGEMENT

If you want to become a domestic goddess or god, it's not that hard. Just follow a few simple rules for creating an orderly routine that will turn housekeeping into an art form. Establishing priorities and setting realistic goals in your daily schedule are essential. Clean the rooms in which you spend the most time and those where cleanliness is a priority – the kitchen, bedroom(s) and bathroom(s). You can let everything else go, at least for a while. Write down what needs to be done that day, do it, then tick it off.

Housekeeping: a state of mind

If you can change the way you think around the home, you will save yourself a lot of time and effort keeping your house clean and tidy/neat. Adopt the key attitudes below and you and your home will instantly benefit.

Neat Living Make this your new mantra. Being neat is a state of mind that will become a lifestyle! Do not let things accumulate on tables, worktops or in the sink, but put everything back in its proper place as you go along. Put dirty clothes in the laundry basket and hang up all clothes as soon as you've taken them off (if they are still clean). Avoid the urge to drop things or put things down where they don't belong, and don't let your family do so either. There will be no one to pick them up but you, and by leaving them you create a mountain of work for yourself.

Do it now, not later Put away newspapers, magazines and similar items as you go along. Don't leave it for later in the day. It will always look worse then. Later can easily become tomorrow, or the next day, and then next week – resulting in a pile of mess and chaos.

Think ahead A useful tip rule is to keep a list of supplies that you need to buy, which can be added to when you see that you've run out of – or preferably before you run out of – essential household items.

GETTING INTO A ROUTINE

In order to keep your housework under control, you need to create a system that makes sense for you, your home and the people you live with. The demands of a large house will not be the same as those of a studio flat/ apartment; and the home of a full-time working couple will not need the same upkeep as a house occupied by a family with two children and a dog. You may have hours to spend each day on keeping your home clean and tidy, or you may only have a few hours during your busy working week. Whatever your lifestyle, however, the housework basics are the same.

Essential daily tasks

If you don't have time to do the more arduous jobs around the home, simplify your routine as much as possible by doing only the essential daily tasks. These entail keeping the bathroom(s), bedroom(s) and kitchen cleaned.

Bathroom(s) Clean surfaces and taps/faucets with a cloth soaked in an antibacterial/disinfectant bathroom cleaner or multi-surface spray. To avoid the build-up of scum, wipe down the shower cubicle or bath with a sponge or cloth after each use. Spraying shower cubicles with a specialist shower spray will prevent the build-up of limescale/mineral deposits. A scummy bath or shower is not inviting to use. Hang wet towels to dry, but if they are sopping wet, change them. Your facecloth may need to be changed daily for hygienic purposes.

Bedroom(s) Make the beds first thing in the morning, but try to air them for a while first. Ventilate the bedrooms for at least half an hour every day, if you can.

Kitchen Keep the kitchen clean, dishes washed and food cupboards well stocked at all times. Clean pots and pans as you go along or stack them in the dishwasher. Even if you haven't got a full load, run a rinse cycle to prevent food from crusting over or rinse them under the tap/faucet. Put out clean dish towels and cleaning utensils every day.

Floors Clean the floors in high-use areas, such as the kitchen and hallway/entryway, especially if you have children or pets. Sweep, damp mop or vacuum as necessary.

Foods Always keep some fresh vegetables and fruit available for a quick, healthy meal, whenever time is short.

General cleaning Cleaners/maids can be expensive, so if you can't afford domestic help once a week, try to arrange to share one with a friend. Choose the most arduous tasks for the professional to do, such as cleaning windows.

Laundry Try to do a little bit of laundry – whether it's washing, drying or ironing – twice a week, before it becomes an overwhelming chore. However, to save fuel and money, wait until you have a full wash load before firing up the washing machine.

Rubbish bins/trash cans Empty kitchen and bathroom waste every day, as a matter of hygiene.

WEEKLY TASKS

Each of these jobs should be tackled at least once a week, some of them more often. Try to establish a weekly routine for these chores so you have a clear idea of what needs to be done on which day.

- Change bed linens.

- Toss pillows into a hot tumble dryer for about 15 minutes to freshen them and eliminate dust mites.

- Change bath towels twice a week.

- Vacuum carpets and rugs twice a week; floors and upholstered furniture weekly.

- Wash all hard-surface floors, such as stone, marble and slate, using a specialized floor cleaner.

- Dust all surfaces and objects that can be dusted, including pictures (don't forget the tops), mirrors, light fixtures and light bulbs.

- Wipe all fingerprints or smears from doorknobs, woodwork, telephones and computer keyboards. Use a soft cloth and an anti-bacterial/disinfectant spray.

- Clean the entire bathroom: toilet, basin, bath, taps/faucets, floor, wall tiles, toothbrush holders and all fixtures and cabinets.

- Clean the entire kitchen: clean the refrigerator; wipe off the cooker (oven and hob) and other appliances inside and out; clean sinks, tables and worktops; wash splashbacks; scrub the floor.

- Clean the oven linings if they are washable – catalytic linings shouldn't be scrubbed. You may need to clean the interior more often, depending on usage.

- Wash out and disinfect rubbish bins/trash cans, as germs accumulate there.

- Do grocery and household shopping once a week. If you keep a rolling shopping list of what you need for the next meals and which household items you have run out of, this should be easy. Attach your list to a pin board in the kitchen and write down what you need to buy when you think of it. Pick up fresh fruit and vegetables as you need them during the week.

- Miscellaneous jobs: for example, cleaning out a kitchen drawer, going through and discarding old cosmetics, throwing out medicines that have expired and so on.

MONTHLY TASKS

Some of these jobs will need to be tackled once a month, others slightly less frequently.

• Wash mirrors and glass panels once a month.

• Launder all bed linens including mattress covers, blankets, pillow covers, quilts and duvets/comforters at least once every three months.

• Turn most frequently used mattresses every four to six months – flip from bottom to top as well as from side to side. You will need help with this.

• Vacuum the mattresses when you flip them.

• Launder pillows according to the instructions on the labels/tags.

• Clean the cooker/range-top hood every two to four months.

• Wax or condition floors every three to six months, depending on use.

• Go through drawers, cupboards and wardrobes frequently to throw out what you no longer use and to clean anything that's become sticky. Hang moth-repellent strips/moth cakes in wardrobes and drawers. Get into the habit of tackling one drawer or cupboard a week in rotation, particularly in the bathroom and kitchen, until they are all done.

• Clean and polish metal household items at least every three to six months. Make sure you use the appropriate product for the metal: silver polish should not be used on brass or pewter.

ANNUAL TASKS

These tasks will need to be dealt with once every six to twelve months, depending on usage.

• Clean lamps, chandeliers and other light fittings once a year or more often if they are unusually dusty.

• Clean all wall surfaces, such as panelling and plaster, at least twice a year. You will probably need to remove finger marks/smudges from walls more frequently. This can be done using a cloth/rag moistened with a detergent solution.

• Clean your storage areas once a year. Invest in a good metal filing cabinet or plastic stacking baskets to store archival files and mementos. Get out of the habit of keeping old boxes that won't be used.

• Move all large appliances, such as the refrigerator, and vacuum and damp mop beneath and behind them at least once a year.

• Shampoo upholstery and carpeting (or call in a professional service) every one to two years, depending on the area's usage. A carpeted bathroom or dining room will need shampooing at least once a year.

• Oil or condition skirting boards/baseboards once every six to twelve months.

• Wash windows and screens at least twice a year.

• Dry-clean or wash window treatments, such as curtains/drapes and fabric blinds/Roman shades, every year.

• Go through your collection of books, CDs, videos and DVDs and dispose of what you no longer want or sell them online. Alternatively, charity shops or public libraries will be happy to take them off your hands.

• Go through your clothes; if you haven't worn an item in the last two years, it's time for it to go. If you don't make room for the new, nothing new will come into your life. And if it does, you won't have a place for it!

CLEANING
BASICS

GETTING THE JOB DONE

In order to keep your home clean and sparkling, you need to have some basic cleaning tools and products. You will also need to know how to carry out basic techniques, such as dusting and mopping, to keep your house in top condition. Before you start, make sure you have all the cleaning materials you need close by.

Cleaning Products

• Use cleaning products only on the surfaces and in the manner recommended on the label.

• Don't use a harsh cleaner when a mild all-purpose product will do the job.

• When mixing solutions, pour in the water before the cleaning product/cleanser so you don't risk splashing the undiluted product on surrounding surfaces.

• A concentrated cleaner is more effective diluted than straight out of the bottle.

• Always test a new product on a small area before using it.

• To save time, put together a basic cleaning kit composed of products you need to clean the kitchen and the rest of the house. Every home is different, so go from room to room in your own home, making a list of all the cleaning products you are going to need. It's a good idea to have a specific cleaning kit in areas of high use, such as the kitchen, the bathroom and the utility room or laundry (if you are lucky enough to have one).

BASIC CLEANING KIT

* Absorbent paper towels

* All-purpose household cleaner

* Ammonia

* Anti-mildew tile and bath/tub cleaner

* Bicarbonate of/baking soda

* Disinfectant cleaner

* Furniture polish

* Isopropyl or rubbing alcohol

* Large and small nylon brushes

* Lint-free cotton cloths

* Micro-fibre cloth

* Non-chlorine bleach

* Nylon scrubbing pad

* Plastic caddy organizer with a handle

* Sponge

* Squeegee

* Washing-up/dish-washing liquid

* White vinegar

* Window cleaner

HOMEMADE CLEANERS

In addition to knowing which cleaning products you need for each room and surface in your home, it's a good idea to be able to create your own cleaning solutions from common household ingredients. The following all-purpose disinfectant cleaners are generally safe to use on most surfaces.

Mild All-purpose Cleaner

• Mix 4 tablespoons bicarbonate of/baking soda with 1 litre/quart warm water.

• Wipe the surface or item, then rinse.

Concentrated All-purpose Cleaner

Do not use the following solutions on aluminium, marble, porcelain or crystal.

• Add 1 tablespoon each of ammonia and liquid laundry detergent to 500 ml/1 pint warm water and stir well.

• Alternatively, add 125 ml/½ cup washing soda to 4 litres/1 gallon warm water.

Semi-abrasive Cleaner

This will remove difficult stains on various surfaces in your home and can be used as an alternative to specialized scouring powders.

• Make a thick paste with bicarbonate of/baking soda and water. Apply to the surface with a sponge or a cloth/rag.

Window Cleaner

• Fill a spray bottle nearly to the top with half water and half rubbing alcohol. Top up with household ammonia and shake lightly.

• Spray on the window, then wipe with a dry, lint-free cloth.

Detergent Solution

This solution is good for cleaning grease or water-soluble stains on most surfaces.

• Mix 1 teaspoon washing-up/dish-washing liquid or detergent powder (containing no bleaches or strong alkalis) with 250 ml/1 cup warm (not hot) water.

• Dampen a white cloth/rag in this solution and carefully rub out the stain until it is gone. Rinse well with clear water.

Ammonia Solution

This is effective in cleaning stubborn floor stains, as well as kitchen appliances and painted wall surfaces. Caution should be used when applying to marble.

• Mix 1 tablespoon clear household ammonia with 125 ml/½ cup water.

• Dampen a white cloth/rag in the solution and carefully rub the stain until it is gone. Once it has gone, rub the area with vinegar solution (see below) to avoid any possibility of skin irritation.

Vinegar

Used on glass, mirrors, laminates and chrome, vinegar is an excellent disinfectant, cleaner and hard-water stain remover.

• Mix 1 part/⅓ cup white vinegar with 2 parts/⅔ cup water. Apply with a cloth/rag.

DUSTING

When you dust, start at the top of the house and work your way down, remembering that dust falls and settles as you dislodge it. Do one room completely – seeing a newly dusted room will be a great incentive to move on to the next one.

Wood Furniture

• Quickly dust the tops of wooden tables at least every other day. Thoroughly dust once a week.

• For cleaning all wood furniture use an old, soft cotton cloth/rag – old cotton T-shirts are great for this. Synthetic material won't absorb cleaning fluids, you need 100 per cent cotton.

• The simplest way to dust is to wipe the surface with a cotton cloth/rag moistened (not saturated) with clear water. However, this won't condition the wood in any way.

• Dust-removing sprays or cloths/rags can be used on wooden surfaces but avoid oils, which attract more dust and finger prints.

• Dust using a circular motion.

• Make sure you dust under table lamps and knick-knacks.

• Dust intricate furnishings, such as those with carvings, with a small, soft brush, such as a natural-hair artist's brush or a dry, soft toothbrush.

• Clean all cloths/rags and brushes when you have finished.

• Furniture wipes/dusting mitts treated with furniture polish make the task even easier. Keep a box of them in your cleaning kit at the ready.

Glass-topped Tables and Monitor Screens

• Dust glass-topped tables and television screens twice a week with a soft cloth/rag and glass spray cleaner.

• Wipe down computer screens once a week. Check the manufacturer's or retailer's recommendations for special cleaning pads for optical plastic and glass.

Ornaments/Bibelots and Knick-knacks

• Clean all objects twice a week.

• Dampen a soft cloth/rag with water and a few drops of washing-up/dish-washing liquid and use to clean off your porcelain or china figurines.

• Clean crystal objects with glass cleaner.

• Dry dust all books with a soft cloth/rag. Alternatively, use the upholstery nozzle/tip of your vacuum cleaner.

USING A MOP

The following instructions are for wood floors and for the everyday maintenance of tiled and stone floors.

• Mop your wood, tiled and hard floors at least once a week. Heavily soiled areas, such as the hallway, kitchen or bathroom, may need to be cleaned more frequently.

• Sweep the floor with a broom or an anti-static cloth mop or vacuum to remove as much dust and debris as you can before you start the wet mopping process.

• Moisten your mop with clear water and an appropriate cleaner for the type of flooring. (Do not use soap on wood floors; instead, add a drop of wood-cleaning detergent to the water.)

• Mop the floor in a sweeping motion, forwards and backwards; do not make a circular motion.

• Lift the mop between strokes to avoid streaking the floor.

• Between strokes, shake off any dust that has gathered on the mop as you work. The mopping process will pick up any dust left behind by the broom.

• Use this mopping process for general, everyday maintenance of tile and stone floors in high-use areas.

• Choose a mop with a removable head that you can launder. String mops are best. Make sure you clean it regularly, and use bleach in the water to disinfect it.

USING A VACUUM CLEANER

• Keep carpets and rugs in top condition by regular vacuuming. Use doormats at the main entrances to your home to pick up debris from the street. Put castor cups/casters under furniture to protect the carpets and rugs.

• Shampoo your carpets every one to two years depending on whether you have small children and pets. If you have the latter, you may have to shampoo it once every six months.

• Use the floor attachment for bare floors or valuable carpets or rugs.

• For regular carpets, use a turbo/power brush attachment.

• To maintain beautiful wood floors, vacuum them along the grain of the wood, preferably with a cylinder rather than an upright cleaner.

WHICH ATTACHMENT TO USE?

AREA TO BE VACUUMED	VACUUM ATTACHMENT
Cabinets, shelves and books	*all-purpose cleaning head/brush*
Wood, stone, linoleum or vinyl floors	*floor attachment*
Narrow areas, detailing	*radiator brush (if supplied)*
Difficult places to clean	*crevice nozzle/tip*
Skirting/base boards and moulding	*dusting brush or upholstery nozzle/tip*
Upholstery	*upholstery nozzle/tip*

FLOORS

The essential character of a house is revealed in its floors. Whether they are hard wood, tile, stone or laminate, your floors reflect the soul of your home and its fundamental design. A floor provides the depth and expanse to a room – as such, it should be kept clean, uncluttered and gleaming. Knowing how to clean all your floor surfaces is imperative for a well-kept home.

Granite and Stone

• Sweep up loose dirt every day with a brush, dust/anti-static mop or vacuum cleaner. Vacuum thoroughly with a floor brush attachment once a week.

• Clean the floor on a weekly basis using a soft mop and a mild detergent solution. Don't use soap because it may leave a film.

• Wipe up spills immediately as most stone is porous, so it stains easily.

• To remove grease or oil, use a specialized stain remover.

• Protect stone floors with a sealant once every three years.

Hard wood

• Sweep up loose dirt every day with a brush, dust/anti-static mop or vacuum cleaner. Vacuum thoroughly with a floor brush attachment once a week.

• Clean with a specialized wood floor cleaner. Use soapy water on sealed wood.

• Do not use furniture sprays or oils on the floor; they will make it slippery.

Linoleum

A resilient floor covering, linoleum stands up well to the wear and tear suffered by a kitchen floor, making it a perfect choice for this room.

• Sweep up loose dirt every day with a brush, anti-static mop or vacuum cleaner.

• Wash with soapy water and a sponge mop. Rinse with clear water and buff dry.

• You can wax with paste or liquid wax.

Tiles

Unglazed tiled floors don't show wear and tear like wood and marble, which (as long as a suitable treatment is applied) makes them good for kitchen floors.

- Sweep up loose dirt every day with a brush, dust/anti-static mop or vacuum.

- Wash once a week with a mild detergent, water and a soft mop.

Vinyl

- Sweep up loose dirt every day with a brush, dust/anti-static mop or vacuum cleaner. Vacuum thoroughly once a week.

- Mop with a solution made from 125 ml/½ cup ammonia per 4 litres/1 gallon water.

- Mopping vinyl regularly with a clean mop and mild detergent or floor cleaner will take care of most dirt and dust. If you want extra protection against germs, add a few drops of disinfectant to the water.

- Don't use harsh cleaners or paste wax, which leave a film residue.

- To remove scuff marks, use a cloth dipped in neat washing-up/dish-washing liquid.

CARPETS

To prolong the life of your carpets, make sure you vacuum them regularly. Thorough vacuuming at least once a week, and more often in heavy traffic areas, will remove dirt particles before they become embedded in the pile. Shampoo your carpets from time to time. For best results, get your carpet professionally cleaned.

Spot Prevention

• To prevent dirt from outside the home getting onto your carpet, place doormats/absorbent mats at all the entrances to your home. To be truly effective they need to be long enough for you to walk across and brush off your shoes as you enter.

• Shake the mats outside and away from where people walk to prevent the dust from being brought back in.

• Clean high-traffic areas occasionally with a dry carpet powder or shampoo. Keep absorbent cloths or paper towels and cleaning solutions on hand for a quick response to spills and accidents.

Spot Removal Basics

• Act quickly whenever anything is dropped or spilled. Remove as much of the spill as quickly as possible using absorbent cloths or paper towels.

• Always work inwards from the edge of the spill to prevent spreading it.

• Do not rub a spill as it may cause the spot to spread or distort the pile.

• Blot up liquid spills with paper towels or an absorbent towel. For a liquid spill, pour sparkling/soda water sparingly over the area; the bubbles will cause more of the spilled substance to rise to the surface, which should then be blotted quickly.

• Scoop up solid spills with a spoon or the end of a blunt knife.

• When the spill has been removed, most spots can be dealt with effectively using the foam from the suds of a solution of water and a mild detergent or carpet shampoo. Otherwise, use the recommended stain remover (see pages 34–35).

• For a wool carpet, or any wool blend, only use products that specify 'suitable for use on wool carpets'.

• Never overwet or soak the carpet. After cleaning, blot as dry as possible with paper towels.

• Remove any remaining stain with carpet shampoo or commercial stain removers, following the relevant instructions.

• Finally, rinse with clear warm water, either by spraying the water onto the carpet, taking care not to get it too wet, or by patting it on with a clean white cloth/rag or paper towels. Then blot dry thoroughly.

• Once dry, brush the pile back with the brush attachment of your vacuum cleaner.

• To raise the pile of a crushed carpet, cover the area with a damp cloth/rag and hold a hot iron over the cloth. Brush up to lift the pile when the carpet is dry.

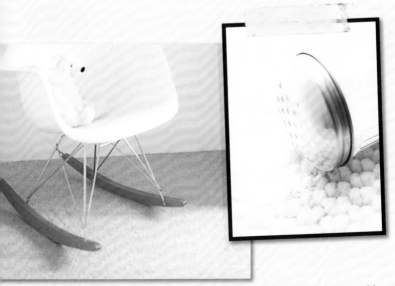

SPOT REMOVAL CHART FOR CARPETS

ITEM	STEP 1	STEP 2	STEP 3
	(order of treatment)		
Alcoholic beverages	1	2	~
Bleach*	1	3	~
Blood	1	2	12
Bolognese sauce	4	2	~
Butter	4	2	~
Candle wax	5	14	9
Chewing gum	5	4	~
Chocolate	2	3	6
Coffee	1	2	4
Colas and soft drinks	1	2	~
Cooking oils	4	2	~
Cream	2	4	~
Curry	13	12	~
Egg	4	2	~

CLEANING AGENT

1. Sparkling/soda water or cold still water
2. Detergent solution or carpet shampoo solution
3. Ammonia solution
4. Dry-cleaning solvent
5. Chill with ice cubes in a plastic bag, then pick or scrape off
6. Vinegar solution
7. Warm water
8. Clear nail polish remover (preferably acetone)
9. Alcohol or methylated/mineral spirits, turpentine
10. Rust remover
11. Specialized absorbent cleaner
12. Professional cleaning
13. Laundry Borax solution (15 ml/1 tablespoon Borax to 500 ml/2 cups warm water)
14. Absorbent paper towels and iron

* Unlikely to be removed

ITEM	STEP 1	STEP 2	STEP 3
Floor wax	4	2	~
Fruit juice	1	2	9
Gravy and sauces	7	2	~
Ink (fountain pen)	1	2	~
Ink (ballpoint)	4	9	2
Ink (felt tip)	7	2	8
Ketchup	7	2	~
Lipstick	4	2	~
Milk	7	4	2
Mustard	2	~	~
Nail polish	8	4	2
Oil and grease	4	2	~
Paint (latex)	1	2	4
Paint (oil)*	9	4	12
Rust	4	2	10
Salad dressing	2	4	~
Shoe polish	4	2	~
Soot	4	2	3
Tar	4	~	~
Tea	1	2	4
Urine (fresh)	1	2	~
Vomit	2	~	~
Wine	1	2	~
Unknown material	4	11	2

UPHOLSTERY

Regular vacuuming of upholstered furniture will help prevent the accumulation of dirt. Do so once a week.

Spot Removal Basics

• Remove excess dirt promptly by scraping off any residue with a blunt/dull knife or spoon, or blotting up spills with paper towel or an absorbent cloth.

• Make sure you pre-test a cleaning solution in an inconspicuous spot before using it on the upholstery.

• Do not remove the cushion from its cover.

• Do not rub the spot; use a soft, white cloth or a clean sponge to apply the relevant cleaning solution.

• Rinse with a damp sponge, then dry immediately with a soft dry cloth.

• If the spot persists, call a professional upholstery cleaner.

Spot Removal Tips

Blood Because blood coagulates, it must never be in contact with anything warm or hot. To clean, mix 1 teaspoon mild detergent or upholstery shampoo with 250 ml/1 cup tepid water. Or, mix one tablespoon ammonia with 125 ml/½ cup water. Apply either solution to the spot with a clean cloth and pat/ tamp dry. Then sponge with clear water and pat/tamp dry.

Chewing gum, ink Sponge with a small amount of dry-cleaning solvent. Blot with a cloth or paper towels.

Chocolate, earth/soil Mix 1 teaspoon mild detergent or upholstery shampoo with 250 ml/1 cup tepid water. Apply to the spot with a clean cloth and pat dry. Then, mix one tablespoon ammonia with 125 ml/½ cup water. Apply to the spot with a clean cloth and pat/tamp dry. Apply the detergent and water solution to the area again. Sponge with clear water and pat/tamp dry.

Coffee, cola drinks Mix 1 teaspoon mild/very gentle detergent or upholstery shampoo with 250 ml/1 cup tepid water. Apply to the spot with a clean cloth and pat/tamp dry. Alternatively, mix 1 part/⅓ cup white vinegar with 2 parts/⅔ cup tepid water. Apply to the spot with a clean cloth and pat/tamp dry. Sponge with clear water and pat/tamp dry.

Nail polish Daub with nail polish remover and pat/tamp dry. Or, mix 1 teaspoon mild/very gentle detergent or upholstery shampoo with 250 ml/1 cup tepid water and blot with a clean cloth. Sponge with clear water and pat/tamp dry.

Soft drinks (other than cola), wine Mix 1 teaspoon mild detergent or upholstery shampoo with 250 ml/1 cup tepid water. Apply to the spot with a clean cloth and pat dry. Then mix 1 part/⅓ cup white vinegar with 2 parts/⅔ cup water. Apply to the spot with a clean cloth and pat/tamp dry.

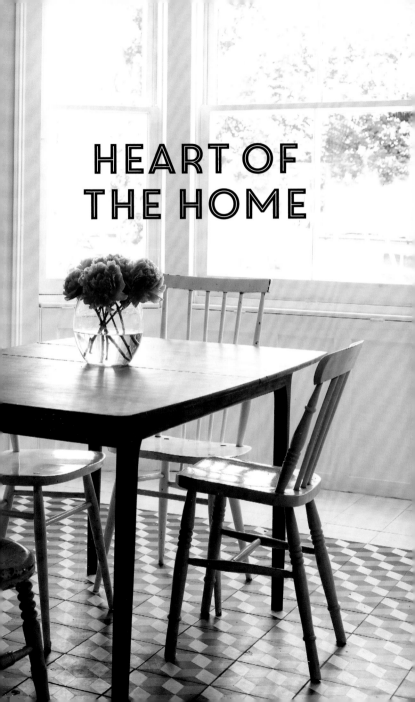

HEART OF THE HOME

GLEAMING KITCHENS

Your kitchen is the heart of your home – where your family's food is prepared, stored, mixed and measured. Make it a special place, suited to your convenience, so you always know where to find what you need. Keep the pots, pans, worktops and chopping blocks meticulously cleaned and you can look forward to donning your apron and whipping up a delicious feast with ease whenever you like.

THE DAILY ROUTINE

If time is short, then the kitchen is the one room that should be kept clean over and above all the others. Food scraps, dirt and grime must be dealt with to keep what is the hub of the home clean and germ-free. Establish a definite routine based on your needs and those of your family, so your kitchen remains neat, as well as stress-free around mealtimes. It is fun to bake chocolate chip cookies with your five year old ... but only if you've organized yourself ahead of time so you can stay one step ahead of your baby Escoffier!

Kitchen Basics

• It's important to begin your day with spotlessly clean utensils and clean work surfaces.

• Change dish towels daily or as necessary.

• Glasses, dishes and sharp knives should be put away after use to avoid nasty accidents and breakages.

• Take a quick look in your refrigerator to check what you will need for meals that day or week. Keep an ongoing list of fresh food and store-cupboard/pantry items you require, so you have a complete list for the next time you do your weekly shop.

• Store all kitchen cleaning products in their caddy within easy reach of appliances. An ideal place is under the kitchen sink, although if you have young children ensure the cupboard has secure child locks. It may be better to store cleaning products and other chemicals out of reach if the family is young.

• Clean up after every meal; clean work surfaces with a cloth dampened with hot soapy water or an anti-bacterial/disinfectant spray for tougher food spills.

• Wipe down the oven door and hob/top of the cooktop after each use. This can be done with a cloth or paper towels dampened with a multi-surface cleaner.

• Empty rubbish bins/trash cans and reline them at the end of every day. Put spare folded plastic rubbish/trash bags at the bottom of the bin/can before relining, so they are ready when you need them next.

• When preparing meals, keep a small receptacle handy for discarding cooking waste/refuse, such as trimmed fat, asparagus stalks, chicken bones and so on.

KITCHEN APPLIANCES

The kitchen remains the central part of the home. Appliances vary from house to house depending on individual needs. The latest kitchen appliances are convenient and easy to use and help us in our everyday tasks, but to get the best use out of them they must be cleaned regularly. Get into the habit of wiping down the exterior of all appliances after each use and cleaning the interiors regularly, according to the manufacturer's instructions.

REFRIGERATOR

Your refrigerator needs to be kept rigorously clean and hygienic. Here are the basic recommendations for upkeep.

Daily

• Check all fresh food items for spoilage and throw out anything that has gone off/spoiled.

• Check use-by/expiration dates on cheese, eggs and milk; discard any items that have expired.

• Wipe up liquid spills or food particles with a scrupulously clean, damp cloth – not the one used to clean work surfaces or the floor!

• Store all leftover foods in sealable, airtight glass or plastic containers.

• Wipe the door handle. For stubborn stains, use an anti-bacterial/disinfectant spray or a paste made from 2 parts/⅔ cup bicarbonate of/baking soda and 1 part/⅓ cup water.

Weekly

• Clean the inside of the refrigerator with a sponge and hot, soapy water.

• Remove the shelves and wash them with hot water and washing-up/dish-washing liquid. Rinse well and dry.

• Wipe the door compartments with a solution made from 2 tablespoons bicarbonate of/baking soda and 1 litre/quart warm water. Rinse and dry.

• Wash the door seal with warm water and washing-up/dish-washing liquid. Rinse well and dry.

• Remove the salad/produce drawers and wash them in the sink with warm water and washing-up/dish-washing liquid.

• Wash the freezer compartment with a solution made from 2 tablespoons bicarbonate of/baking soda and one 1 litre/quart warm water. Rinse and dry.

Monthly

• Vacuum the condenser coils at the back of the refrigerator if they are exposed.

• Defrost the freezer every 2–3 months. Some freezers today are self-defrosting; but if you don't have one that is, you will need to defrost your freezer manually. To do so, first empty the freezer and turn it off. Put bowls of boiling water inside and as it defrosts wipe out the water and residue with a clean cloth/rag.

HOBS/COOKTOPS AND GRIDDLES

Hobs/cooktops are used frequently, whatever your cooking habits, and soon get grimy from spills, oils and fats. Wipe up spills immediately and wipe down the area daily with a damp cloth. This will keep the hob hygienic and prevent fires or other accidents from occurring.

Cleaning Gas Hobs/Cooktops

• Wait until the hob/cooktop is cool.

• Remove burner surrounds, spillage wells and pan supports and immerse in a hot washing-up/dish-washing liquid solution. You may need to use a cream cleaner and nylon scourer to remove burnt-on dirt. (Check to see if they can go in the dishwasher.)

• Spray hob top with an appropriate cleaner depending on the type of surface.

• Clean metal surrounds with an appropriate metal cleaner. For tough caked-on debris, use an old toothbrush soaked in a cream cleaner and water. Wipe clean.

• Remove control knobs if possible and clean with hot soapy water.

Cleaning Electric Hobs/Cooktops

• Solid hotplates may need cleaning with a cream cleaner or scouring pad.

• To prevent rusting, when clean wipe over with a few drops of vegetable oil applied on kitchen paper or a specialized hob conditioner.

• Don't worry if they smoke slightly when switched on again, this is normal.

Cleaning Glass-topped Hobs/Cooktops

• Wait until the hob is cool.

• Remove light debris with paper towels or a damp cloth.

• Only use a cleaning product recommended by the hob/cooktop manufacturer.

• Remove heavier stains with a specialist hob/cooktop scraper (usually supplied with the hob/cooktop or available from hardware stores).

• After cleaning, use a specialist hob/cooktop conditioner.

• To avoid scratches always use smooth-based pans and wipe the bases before putting them on the hob/cooktop. Do not drag pans across the surface. Make sure your cloths are free from grit before using.

• Wipe up sugar-based spills straight away, the sugar will crystallize and cause pitting on the glass.

Cleaning Gas Griddles

• The cast aluminium griddle has a non-stick coating to ensure easy cleaning. For best results, wash the surface with hot soapy water, rinse and dry.

• Don't use steel wool or coarse scouring pads or powders.

• The non-stick surface needs periodic conditioning. To do so, apply cooking oil and wipe off the excess.

• Don't use metal cooking utensils – they scratch the non-stick coating. Use plastic or wooden ones instead.

OVENS

Clean your oven once a week if you cook every day and every two weeks if you cook less frequently. Having a clean oven helps keep your kitchen sweet-smelling and prevents your food from smelling of yesterday's leftovers.

Cleaning the Outside of the Oven

• For stainless steel panels use a specialized stainless steel cleaner. Remove finger marks with a soft cloth and a few drops of baby oil or rinse aid.

• If your oven panel is glass, spray with a multi-surface cleaner or glass cleaner.

• Soak grill pans, knobs and drip pans in hot, soapy water. Use a stiff brush to remove any burnt-on food residue or grease.

Cleaning the Inside of the Oven

• Your oven should be cleaned according to the type of linings or cleaning systems it has. Refer to your manual for specific directions.

• Enamel linings (untreated) should be cleaned using a specialized oven cleaner.

• Always wear rubber gloves and make sure the kitchen is well ventilated.

• For easy-to-clean areas, use regular detergent or a liquid cleanser. To remove baked-on food, first prise off what you can with a blunt/dull knife. Spray stubborn remaining spots with a commercial or homemade oven cleaner (see right) and use a scouring pad.

• Self-cleaning or catalytic linings: the oven sides are treated with a special vitreous enamel that absorbs grease. They ensure that fat and grease are burnt off and vaporized rather than being deposited on their surface. Heat the oven to a high temperature for about 30 minutes once a week for best results. Avoid detergents.

• Pyrolytic cleaning: Top of the range ovens have a built-in cleaning cycle. The empty oven is heated to a very high temperature for a specific period of time. This turns the dirt to ashes, which can be brushed out easily when the oven is cool.

• Hydroclean system involves pouring water and detergent on the oven floor and heating the oven. The steam loosens dirt, which is wiped away.

• To make the oven easier to clean, put a bowl of water in the oven at a high temperature for about 20 minutes. The steam loosens the dirt, so simply wipe it away. Another tip is to cover the floor and side panels of the oven with a thin paste of bicarbonate of/baking soda and water. During cooking it dries to form a protective layer, which absorbs grease and can be wiped out easily afterwards.

Homemade Oven Cleaner

For use on untreated enamel linings only.

• Wet the inside surfaces of the oven and apply bicarbonate of/baking soda to all the surfaces on a damp cloth. Rub with fine steel wool, then wipe off any grime with a damp cloth or sponge. Repeat if necessary, then rinse well and dry.

• Use a specialized oven cleaner for burned-on mess.

KITCHEN DRAINS

If you follow the advice given below, you will help to keep your drains clean and clear, prevent blockages and unsanitary conditions and also help to avoid any unpleasant smells from developing.

Avoiding Clogged Drains

• Purchase a drain strainer. This fits over the plug hole and allows water to drain through it, but will catch any food particles, which then can easily be thrown away. These are available from hardware stores.

• Grease and oil cause clogging. Make sure you never pour leftover fat down the drain. Instead, pour it into a can or jar, cover well and refrigerate. When it has solidified, throw it away.

• While you are cooking, keep a small pedal bin/mini trash container for food debris close by. Line it with a pedal bin liner/small trashcan liner and use it for discarding your cooking scraps. Likewise, when rinsing your plates and dishes after a meal, make sure you put as many of the leftovers as possible into the bin/mini trashcan to stop food debris getting into the drain. After you have

finished preparing and eating your meal, remove the liner or bag from the bin/mini trashcan, throw it away and replace it with a new one.

• To prevent a build up of grease in the sink and waste pipes, flush once a week with a solution made from 150 g/¾ cup washing soda crystals and 500 ml/2 cups hot water. Alternatively, use a specialized drain cleaner.

Homemade Drain Cleaners for Regular Maintenance

To clean and deodorize Pour 150 g/¾ cup washing soda crystals down the drain and then slowly drip warm water into it. Alternatively, add 150 g/¾ cup washing soda to 4 litres/1 gallon warm water. First pour hot water down the drain, then pour down the washing soda solution, followed by more hot water. Use either method once every 2 weeks to keep the drain clear.

To disinfect/sanitize Mix 175 ml/¾ cup household/chlorine bleach, 1 tablespoon washing powder/powdered laundry detergent and 4 litres/1 gallon warm water. Pour the solution into the sink, let it drain, then rinse with warm water. Do this once a month.

Homemade Cleaners for Clogged Drains

• Pour 150 g/¾ cup washing soda crystals down the drain, followed by 250 ml/ 1 cup white vinegar. Alternatively, mix 2 teaspoons ammonia with 1 litre boiling water and pour down the drain. Use a plunger after either solution.

• Eco-friendly enzymatic drain openers can be put down the drain to unclog it.

BATHROOM
BLISS

BEAUTIFUL BATHROOMS

The measure of a well-kept home can be found in its bathrooms, which should be spotless, germ-free, shiny and sweet-smelling. Keeping you and your family healthy begins by maintaining a bathroom that is devoid of mildew, soap scum and limescale/mineral deposits. This can also become your sacred space, a place to which you can retreat to relax. Make it your haven by filling it with specially chosen products, beautiful scents and fluffy towels.

THE DAILY ROUTINE

It doesn't take much time to keep your bathroom spotless and glowing. For general maintenance, just a few minutes every day will usually suffice. Wipe the shower and basin/sink after each use if you have time. Keep cleaning products tucked away in their caddy inside a cabinet to quickly sanitize the toilet.

Bathroom Basics

• Frequency of cleaning should not vary.

• Use separate cleaning cloths, tools or sponges for those areas with high populations of germs and bacteria – the toilet, toilet lid and floor or walls near the toilet. As a general rule, move from low contamination areas to high ones.

• Frequently used toilets should be cleaned every day. Use a clean cloth/rag and anti-bacterial/disinfectant spray to wipe down the rim of the bowl and seat. Use a brush and a standard toilet bowl liquid or gel cleaner for the toilet bowl. Gels are better because they stay in contact with the bowl for longer.

• Invest in a 'catch-all' for your shower drain – a plastic strainer that goes over the drain to catch hair as you shower. This will prevent the drain from getting blocked.

• Baths/tubs that are used daily should be wiped down daily.

• Keep a plastic squeegee in the shower to wipe off the glass and tiles immediately after showering to prevent nasty water spots from appearing.

• A specialized shower spray will slow down the build-up of limescale/mineral deposits.

- Keep a clean, soft cloth/rag or sponge available to wipe off the basins and any other surfaces, but don't ever use the same one on or around the toilet.

- Store a dry cloth/rag in a cabinet or bathroom cupboard to polish any chrome fixtures after use. If you wipe them straight away, it will prevent water spotting, which is more difficult to remove if left to air dry.

- Keep a mirror cleaner and a disinfectant spray handy.

- In order to maintain good air quality, it is essential to ventilate your bathroom as soon as it has been used. Opening the windows after you shower or have a bath is the best form of ventilation. It's also a good idea to invest in a good extractor fan in the toilet area.

- Air fresheners are effective, too, but nothing beats fresh air.

FIXTURES AND FITTINGS

Your bathroom fittings need to be kept meticulously clean. A bathroom caddy holding all the necessary cleaning products and tools will make this task easier. A freshly scrubbed bathroom is not only inviting, it can become your haven after a hard day.

Toilets

Okay, so it's not the nicest job in the world, but it's easy to do if you have a toilet bowl brush and caddy stored right next to the toilet. Always keep a toilet cleaner closeby to quickly sanitize the toilet on a daily basis.

Routine Maintenance

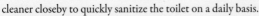

• Clean outside the toilet bowl with washing-up liquid/dish-washing solution or anti-bacterial/disinfectant spray.

• Toilet-bowl cleaners of all sorts will not harm vitreous china toilets.

• For stubborn spots, use neat washing-up liquid/dish-washing liquid and a soft nylon-bristle brush.

• In hard-water areas, use a combined cleaner and limescale/mineral remover.

• Never leave products on for too long otherwise the chemicals could penetrate the surface through worn areas or cracks in the glaze, resulting in discolouration.

• To prevent blockages, pour 150 g/¾ cup washing soda into the toilet bowl, then flush the toilet. Do this once a week.

Disinfecting the Toilet Bowl

• Toilet bowl cleaners should be used daily, or at least once a week.

• Use a long-handled rim brush to clean the rim holes and to clean as far into the trap as possible to prevent limescale/mineral deposits from forming. Alternatively, use a mousse that expands under the rim.

• A toilet block under the rim will keep it smelling fresh and protect against germs.

• Add disinfectant to the toilet bowl and leave for 30 minutes.

• Clean the toilet brush by swirling it around the toilet bowl, then let it stand in a fresh mixture of disinfectant in the toilet bowl for 20 minutes.

• While the brush is soaking, wash the toilet brush stand with a disinfectant cleaner.

• Rinse the brush and replace it in the stand.

Limescale/Mineral Deposit removal

• Daily use of a standard toilet bowl cleaner with built-in limescale/ mineral deposit protection should be sufficient to keep limescale/ mineral deposits at bay. If not, use a specialized limescale remover for sanitary ware or a bleach solution and scrub with a long-handled brush.

• In hard-water areas, keep the holes in the rim clear for proper bowl flushing.

• Homemade limescale/mineral deposit remover: soak a cloth/rag or a paper towel in white vinegar and leave it on the trouble spot for 1 hour. This is effective in softening the limescale/mineral deposit spot for easier removal.

BATHS AND BASINS

There are many styles and types of bath/tubs and basins/sinks from which to choose: porcelain, enamel, fibreglass and acrylic. Nothing looks more inviting than a freshly scrubbed basin/sink or bath/tub. Generally, a quick wipe down after use will suffice to remove scum, but there are also wonderful spray-on cleaners widely available.

Porcelain Enamel Baths/Tubs and Basins/Sinks

• Wash with a gentle, all-purpose cleaner.

• Remove hard-water stains with a solution of 1 part/⅓ cup white vinegar and 1 part/⅓ cup water, or use a specialized limescale/mineral deposit remover for sanitary ware. Rinse thoroughly and dry with a clean cloth/rag.

Fibreglass and Acrylic Baths/Tubs

• Follow the manufacturer's instructions. If they are not readily available, clean regularly with an all-purpose bathroom cleaner.

• For stubborn marks, use a nylon bristle brush and some neat washing-up liquid/dish-washing liquid. Do not use abrasive cleaners.

Stainless Steel Basins/Sinks

• Make a cleaning solution from 4 tablespoons bicarbonate of/baking soda dissolved in 1 litre/quart water. Wipe around the basin using a cloth/rag dipped in this solution. Wipe dry with a clean cloth/rag and polish with a dry cloth/rag.

• Alternatively, clean with an all-purpose powdered cleanser and a soft sponge as necessary, depending on usage.

• Rub lightly with the grain when cleaning.

• For tough streaks and water spots, remove with a cloth/rag dampened with (isopropyl) alcohol, then let air dry.

• Do not use bleach on stainless steel.

TAPS/FAUCETS
AND SHOWERS

As the 'jewels' of your bathroom, your fittings/fixtures should shine. Always wipe taps/faucets and showerheads/shower sets after use to prevent water spots or stains. Taps/faucets are usually made of chrome, which is a plate finish for brass metal. Simple maintenance includes wiping off with a dry cloth/rag after use, and occasional washing with a washing-up/dish-washing liquid solution. Do not use metal polishes, spray polishes or acidic cleaners.

Polished Chrome

• Clean with a washing-up/dish-washing liquid solution and a soft sponge, then dry with a soft, clean cloth/rag.

• Do not use abrasive cleaners. To clean stubborn spots, use undiluted washing-up/dish-washing liquid or a specialized bathroom cleaner.

• Cleaning frequency will depend on usage. Weekly applications give best results.

• To keep shower fittings/fixtures beautiful, always clean and dry them after use. After you've wiped down the wet tiles, use a clean, dry cloth/rag to polish the fittings/fixtures. This should be done after each use to prevent water spots.

• Remove rust or hard-water deposits with any mildly acidic solution, such as a mixture of 1 part/⅓ cup white vinegar or lemon juice and 1 part/⅓ cup water. Alternatively, use a specialized limescale/mineral deposit remover.

Plastic

• If your showerhead/shower set is made of plastic and there is limescale/mineral deposit build-up on it, remove the head/set and soak it in a mixture of 1 part/⅓ cup vinegar and 1 part/⅓ cup water for a few hours. Don't soak polished nickel in the vinegar and water mixture or it will tarnish; use a specialized product instead and check the instructions first.

SHOWER ENCLOSURES

This small space traps moisture and unwanted soap build-up. To prevent scum, wipe showers after each use and clean thoroughly every week.

Routine Maintenance

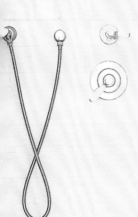

• Wipe off and rinse the shower screen/stall and tiles after every use.

• Wipe off dirt, grime and soap scum as necessary with water and a soft cloth/rag. Don't use any chemicals or abrasive cleaners. If water spots persist using water and a soft cloth/rag, try a small amount of a standard bathroom cleaner or shower spray.

• Counters and walls in shower enclosures and those near baths/tubs and basins/sinks need to be cleaned thoroughly once a week with an all-purpose cleaner to prevent a build-up of scum.

• Spray tiles and shower curtain (if plastic) with a bathroom cleaner. Wipe off, then rinse. Pat/tamp dry.

• To remove mildew from shower curtains, scrub with a bleach solution and rinse well.

INDEX

photography and location credits by page

1, 6 Mark & Sally Bailey's home in Herefordshire. ph Debi Treloar; 2, 24 ph Lucinda Symons; 3 Foster House at www.beachstudios.co.uk. ph Polly Wreford; 4 Hélène & Konrad Adamczewski, Lewes. ph Debi Treloar; 5 l, 20–21, 25 Foster House at www.beachstudios.co.uk. ph Polly Wreford; 5 r ph Claire Richardson; 8-9, 12 The family home of Tine Kjeldsen and Jacob Fossum owners of www.tinekhome.dk. ph Polly Wreford; 11 Bruno et Michèle Viard: location-en-luberon.com. ph Polly Wreford; 13 The home in Norfolk of Laura & Fred Ingrams of Arie & Ingrams Design. ph Debi Treloar; 14 The home of Inger Lill Skagen in Norway. ph Debi Treloar; 15, 23 b, 31 a, 46, 50 i, 51 b, 60 ph Debi Treloar; 16 ph Dan Duchars; 17 ph Sandra Lane; 18 al, 33 l ph Winfried Heinze; 18 ar The home of Netty Nauta in Amsterdam. ph Debi Treloar; 18 b The home of Nicky Sanderson, the co-owner of Lavender Room in Brighton. ph Debi Treloar; 22 bg, 36–7 bg, 43 below ph Kate Whitaker; 22 i, 28 ph William Lingwood; 23 a ph Richard Jung; 26, 29, 45 l, 59 ph Polly Wreford; 27 left, 31 bl The home of Guy & Natasha Hills in London. ph Debi Treloar; 27 r ph Henry Bourne; 31 br Lykkeoglykkeliten. blogspot.com. ph Debi Treloar 33 r, 35 a, 56 ph David Montgomery; 34 bg ph Steve Painter; 34 i ph Jonathan Gregson; 35 bg ph Clare Winfield; 35 b ph Terry Benson; 36 l Caravane by François Dorget. ph Debi Treloar; 36 r ph Gavin Kingcome; 38–39 Home of Rose Hammick and Andrew Treverton, www.marmoraroad.co.uk. ph Polly Wreford; 40, 42, 51 a ph Simon Brown; 41 Stella Willing stylist/designer and owner of house in Amsterdam. ph Debi Treloar; 43 a Khadi & Co., by Bess Nielsen. ph Debi Treloar; 44, 50 bg ph Peter Cassidy; 45 r ph David Brittain; 47 a house in London, architectural design and procurement by Tyler London Ltd, interior design by William W. Stubbs, IIDA. ph Christopher Drake; 49, 63 ph Jan Baldwin; 52–53 The home of Sarah and Mark Benton in Rye. ph Polly Wreford; 54 The home of Charlie and Alex Willcock in West Sussex. ph Polly Wreford; 55 The home of Fiona and Alex Cox of www.coxandcox.co.uk. ph Polly Wreford; 57 Beauty Point and Coast House. ph Polly Wreford; 58 Florence Lim's house in London – architecture by Voon Wong Architects, interior design by Florence Lim Design. ph Christopher Drake; 61 Calvin Tsao & Zack McKown's apartment in New York designed by Tsao &McKown ph Chris Everard; 64 ph Mark Lohman